DECORATIVE ALPHABETS

Stained Glass Pattern Book

BY ED SIBBETT, JR.

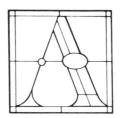

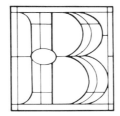

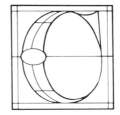

Dover Publications, Inc., New York

Published in Canada by General Publishing Company, Ltd., 30 Lesmill Road, Don Mills, Toronto, Ontario.

Decorative Alphabets Stained Glass Pattern Book is a new work, first published by Dover Publications, Inc., in 1986.

Manufactured in the United States of America
Dover Publications, Inc., 31 East 2nd Street, Mineola, N.Y. 11501

Library of Congress Cataloging-in-Publication Data

Sibbett, Ed.
    Decorative alphabets stained glass pattern book.

    1. Glass painting and staining—Patterns.   2. Alphabet.   I. Title.
TT298.S4854   1986   748.5′022′2   86-13415
ISBN 0-486-25206-X (pbk.)

PUBLISHER'S NOTE

References to church windows made of colored glass place the art of stained glass at least as far back as the fifth century. The art form flourished during the twelfth and thirteenth centuries, when stained glass windows illuminated and decorated most of Europe's finest cathedrals. Recent times have seen many fine examples of both religious and secular stained glass, including its use in the architecture of Le Corbusier and the art of Chagall, Léger and Tiffany.

Ed Sibbett, Jr. is the creator of numerous Dover books of stained glass patterns. For this volume he has rendered the letters of the alphabet in seven different fonts, six accompanied by the numerals 0 through 9. These 60 plates range in style from Gothic to modern, including examples of Art Nouveau, Art Deco and abstract geometric lettering. They lend themselves to many projects: windows, lampshades, mirrors, ornaments, mobiles and any other free-form applications you can think of. A single letter can personalize or monogram a household object; a group of letters or letters and numbers can help you create your own work of art. The work you do with these stained glass patterns is sure to be a graceful and elegant expression of yourself.

This book is intended as a supplement to the standard instruction books now on the market, such as *Stained Glass Craft* by Divine and Blachford, Dover 22812-6. Supplies of glass and other materials, including general instruction books and tools for beginners, can usually be purchased from local craft and hobby stores as listed in your Yellow Pages.

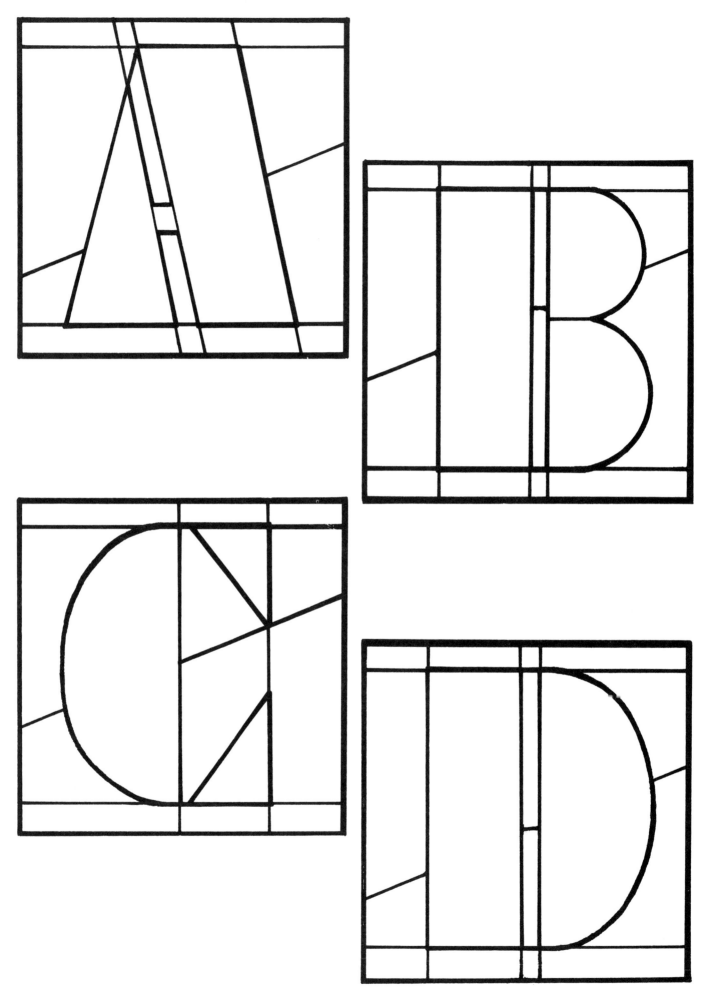

4

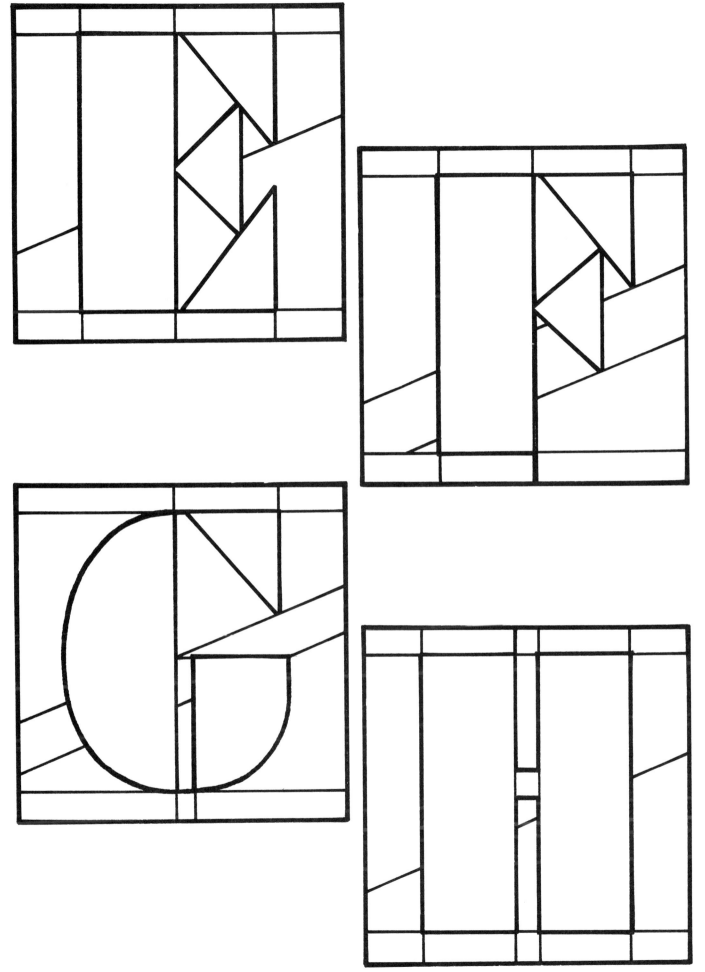

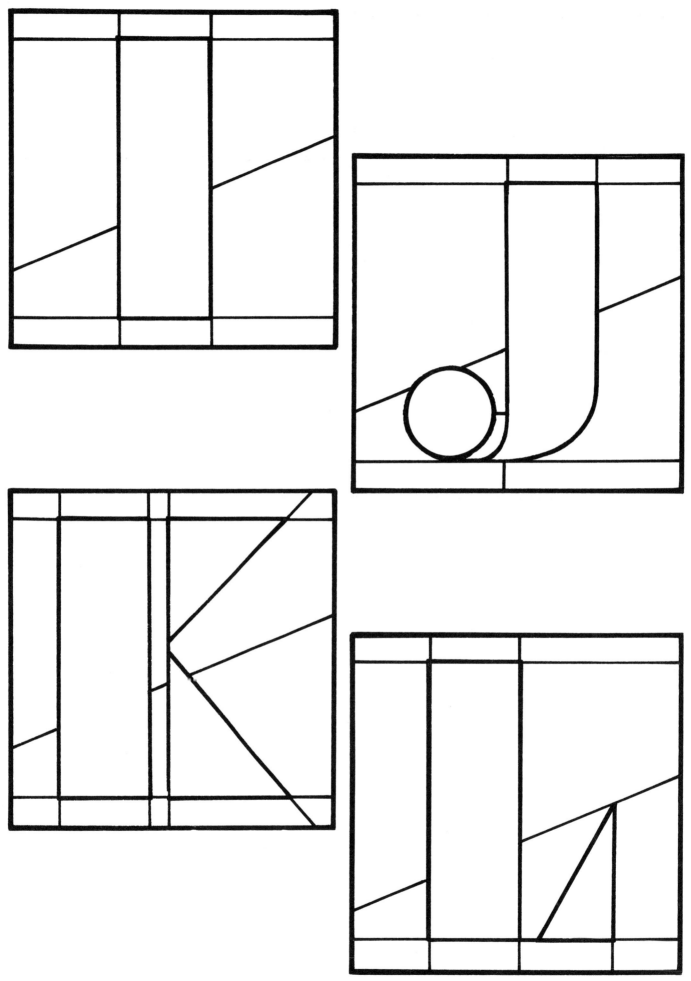

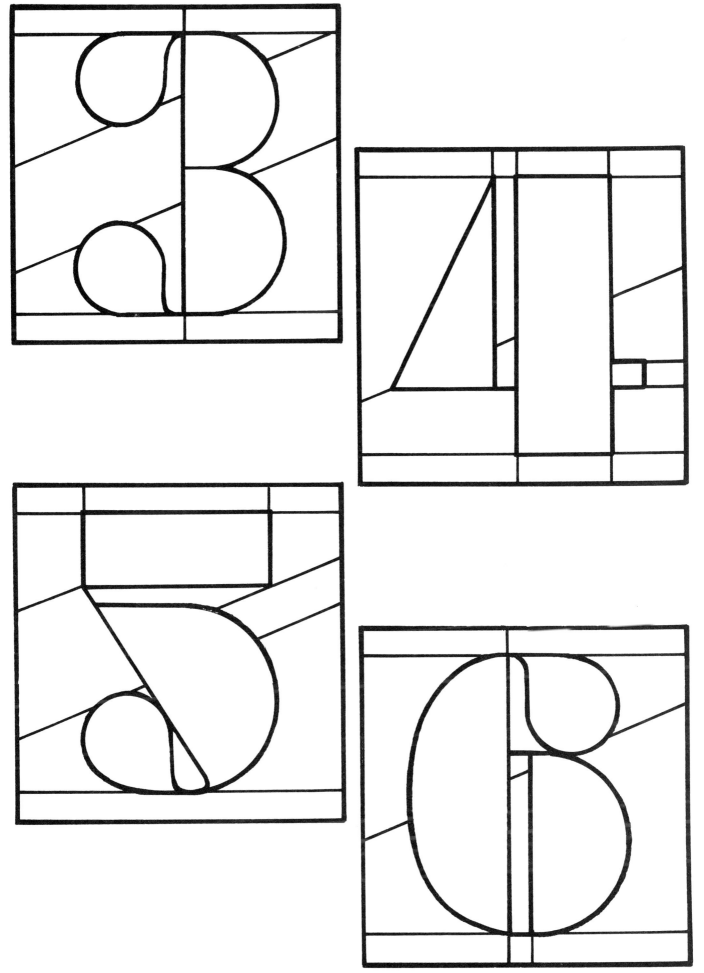

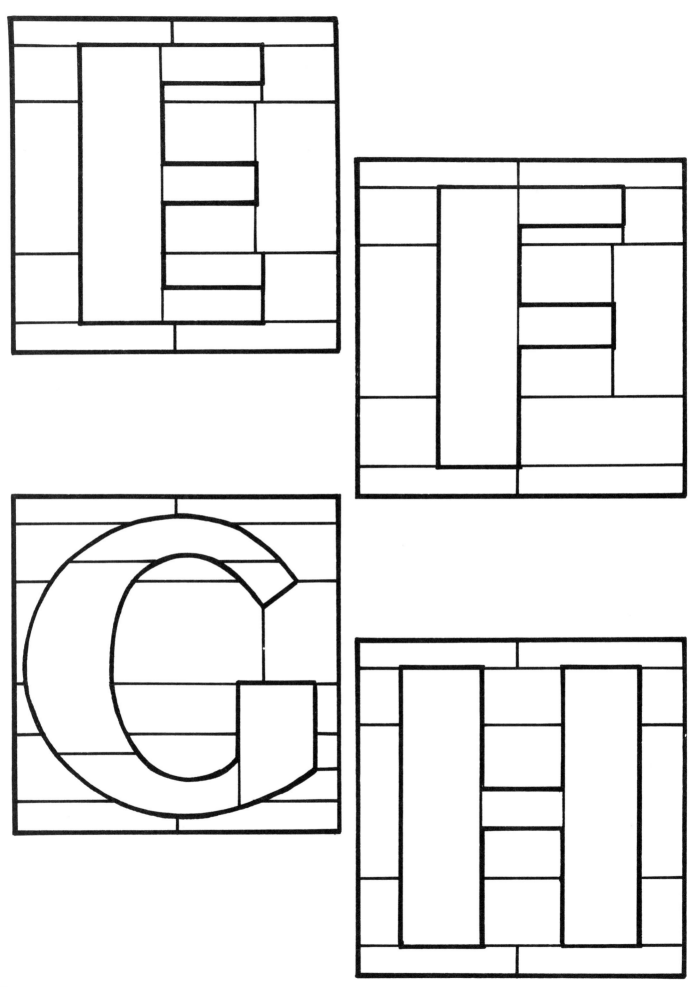

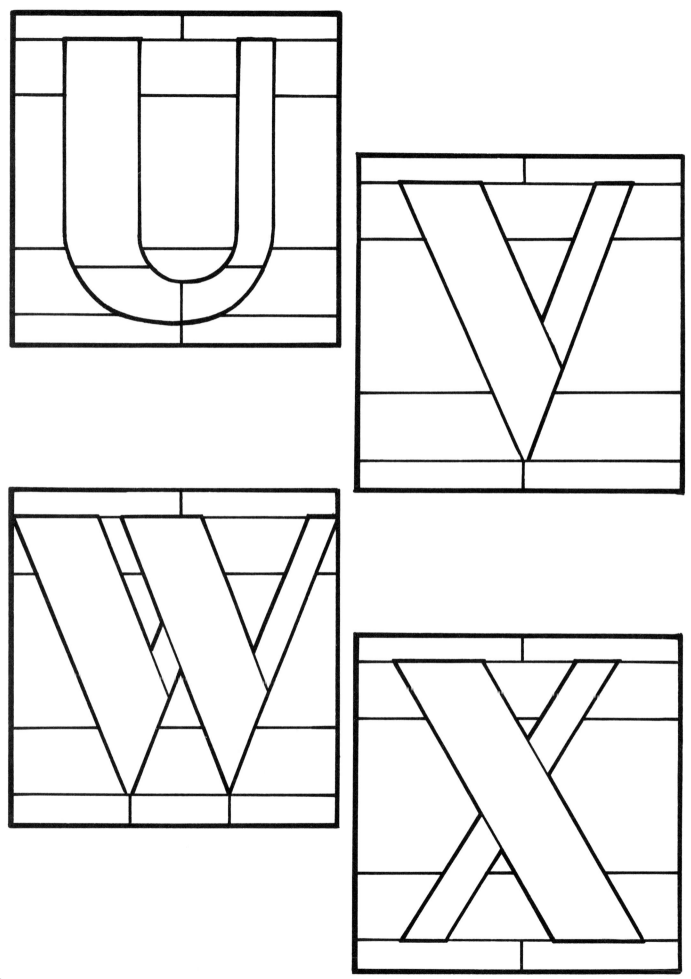

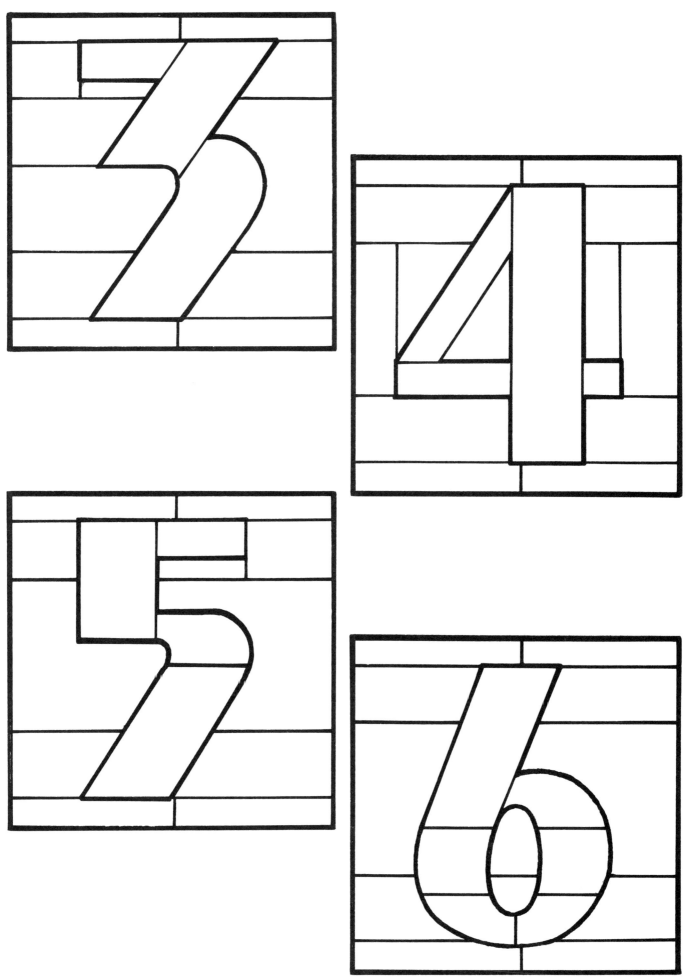

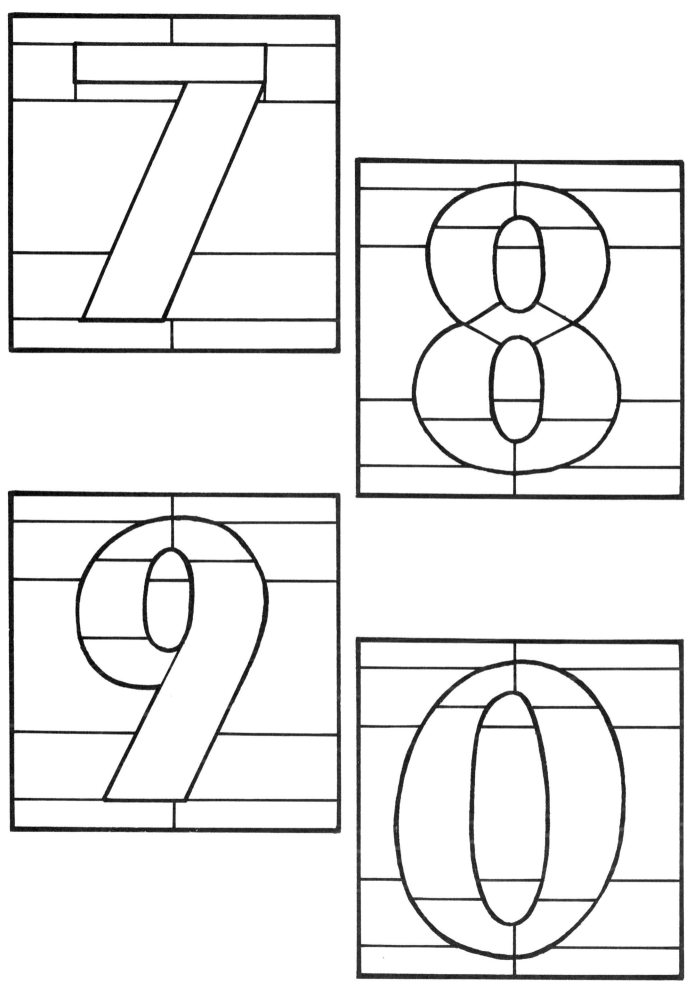

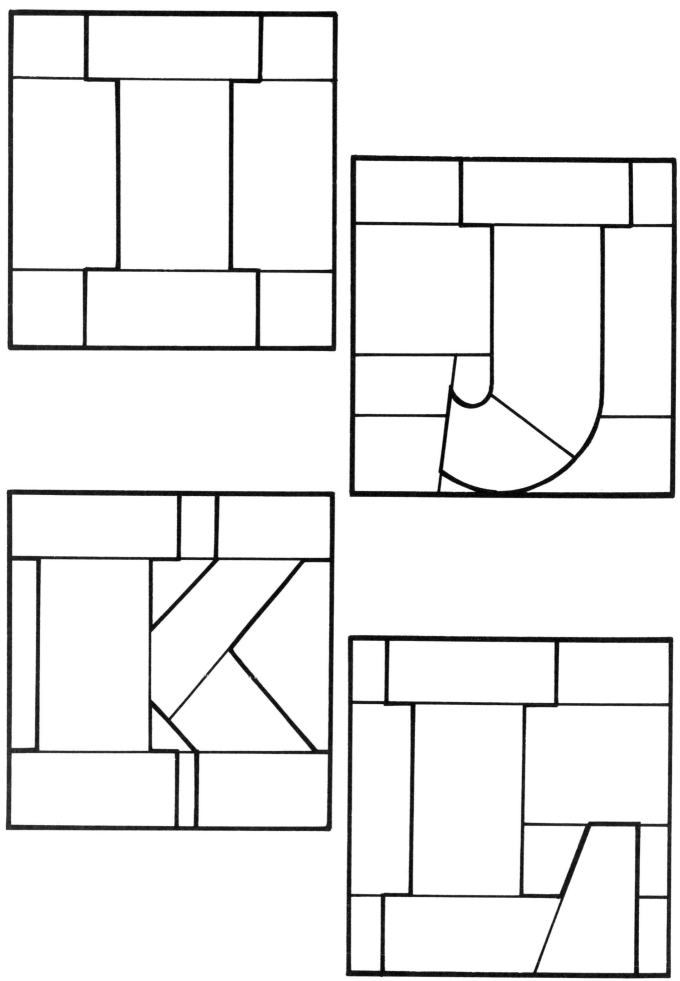

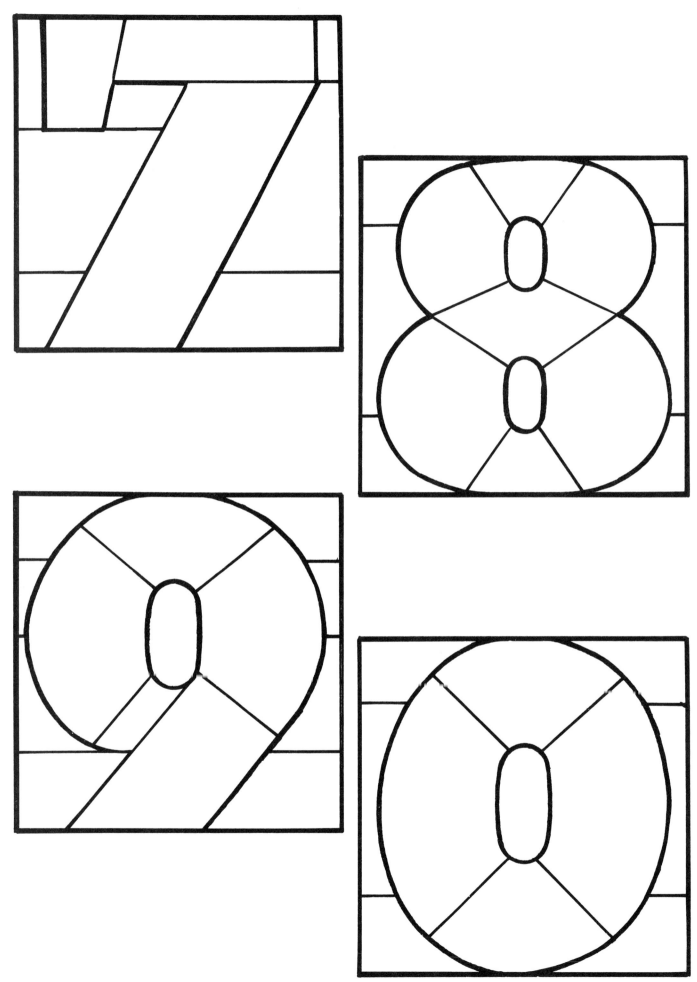

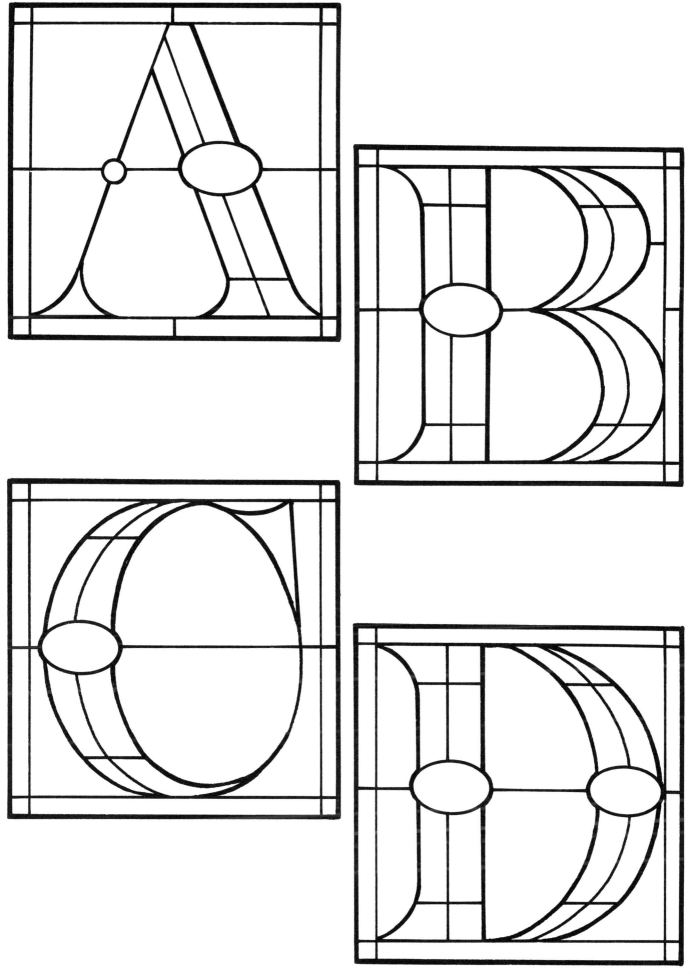

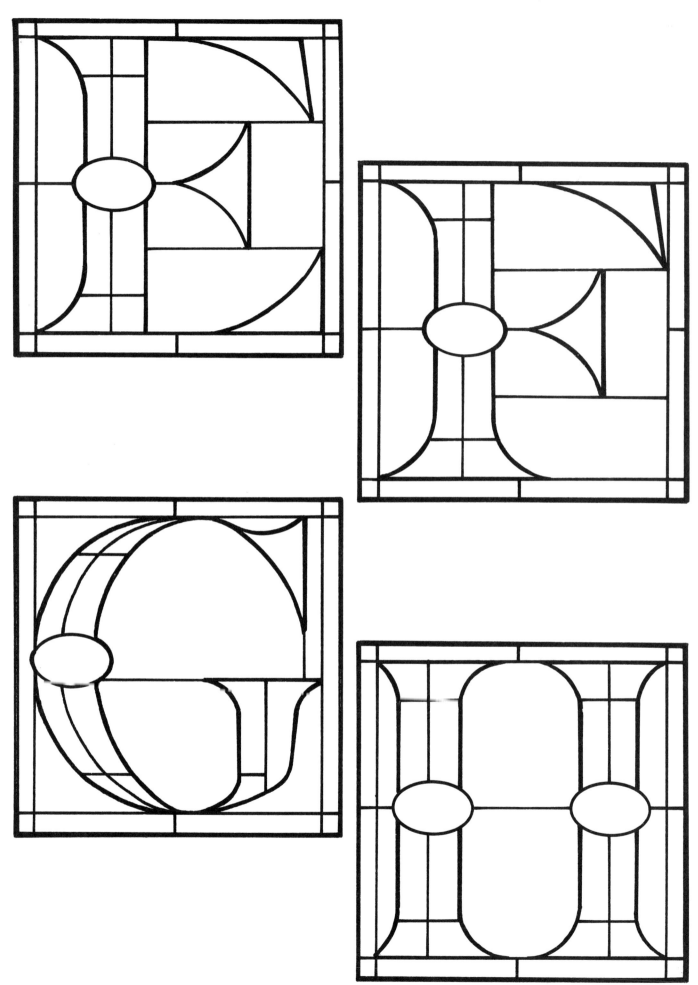

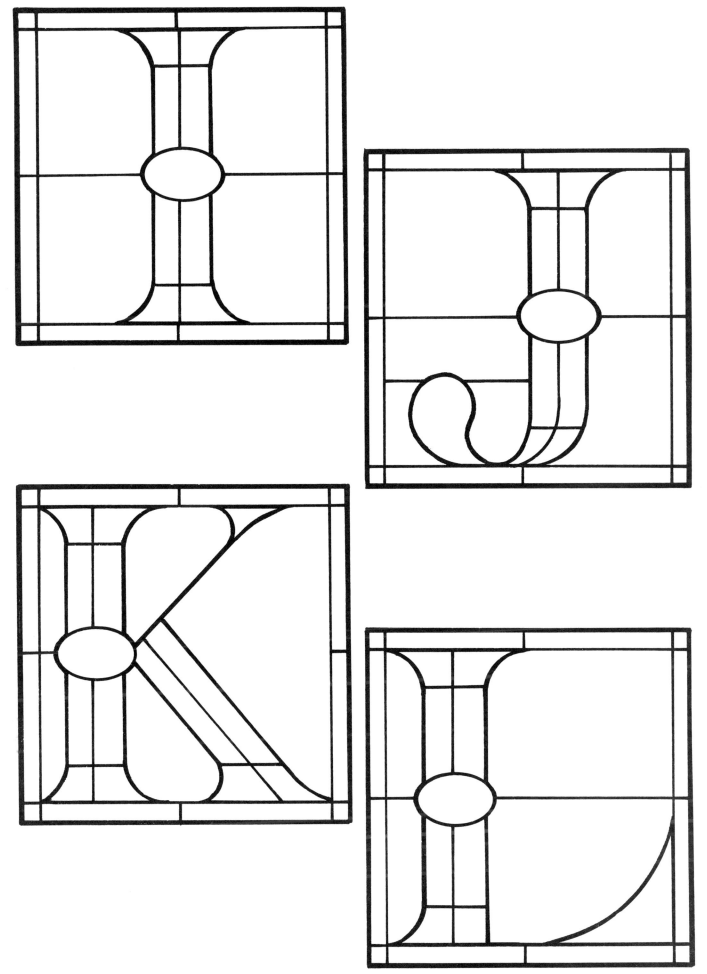

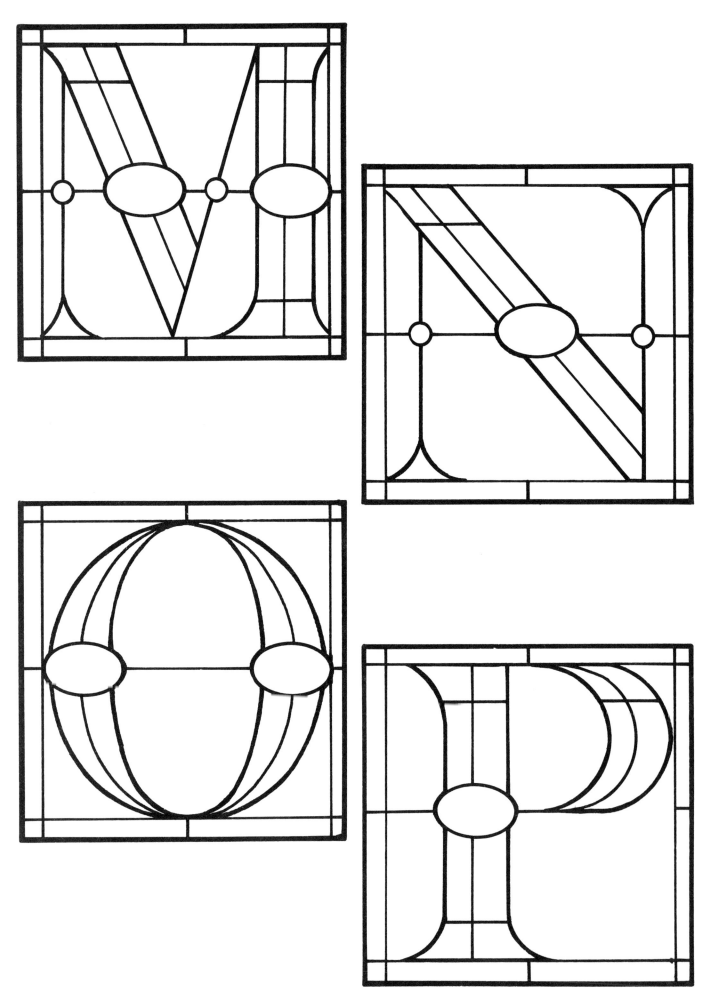

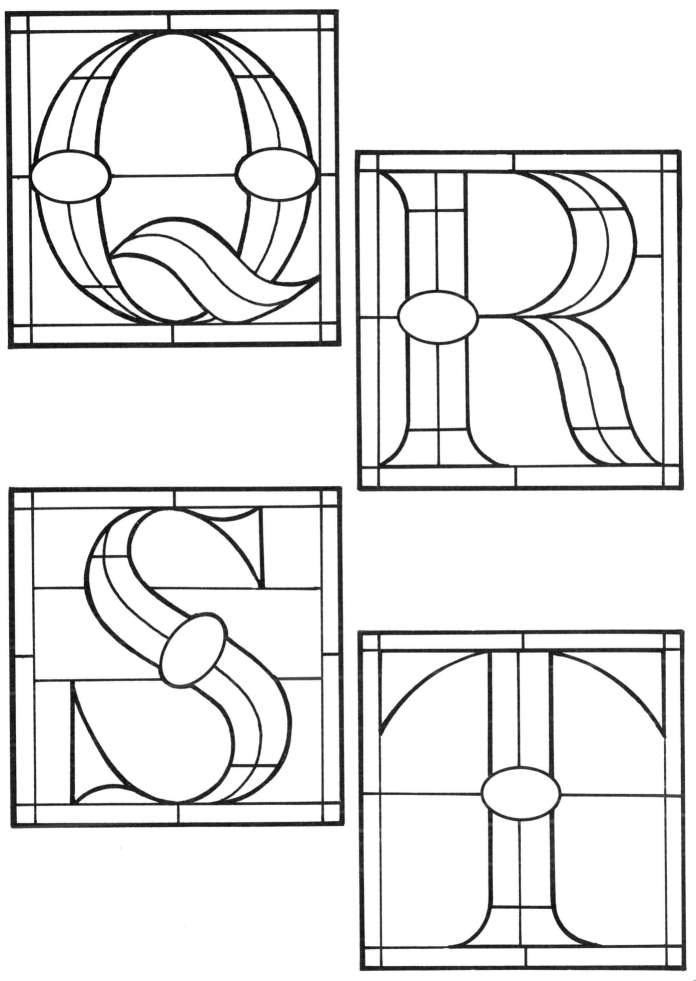

35

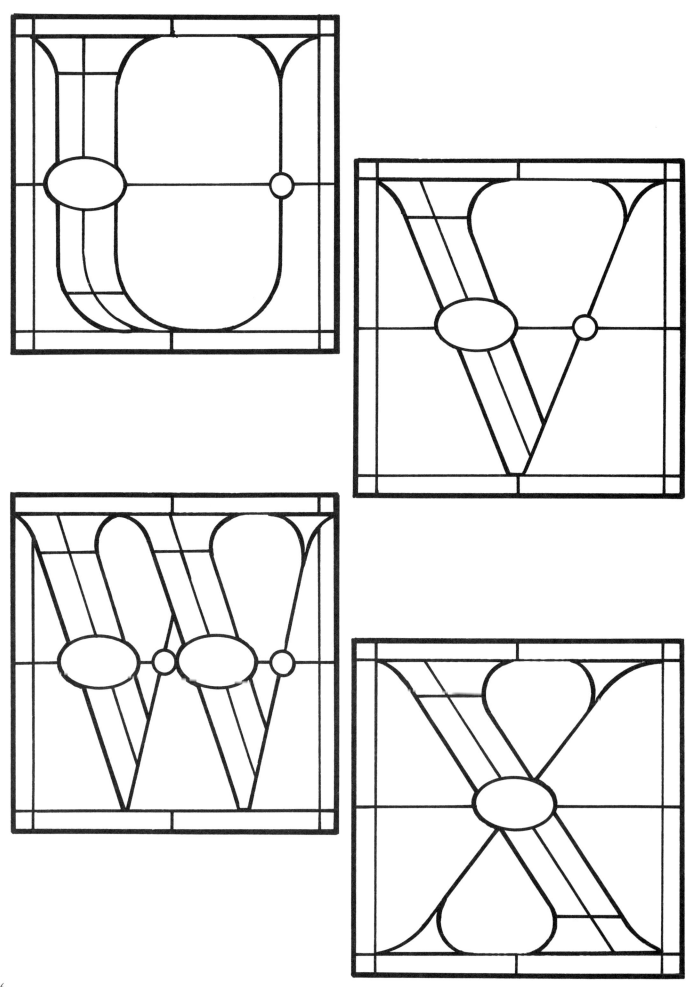

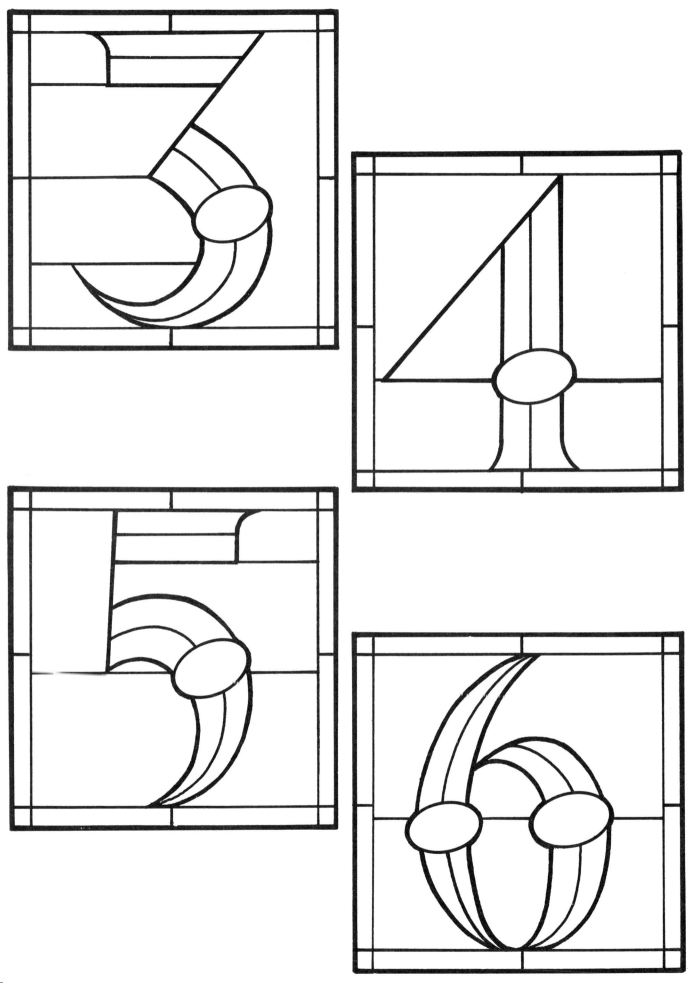

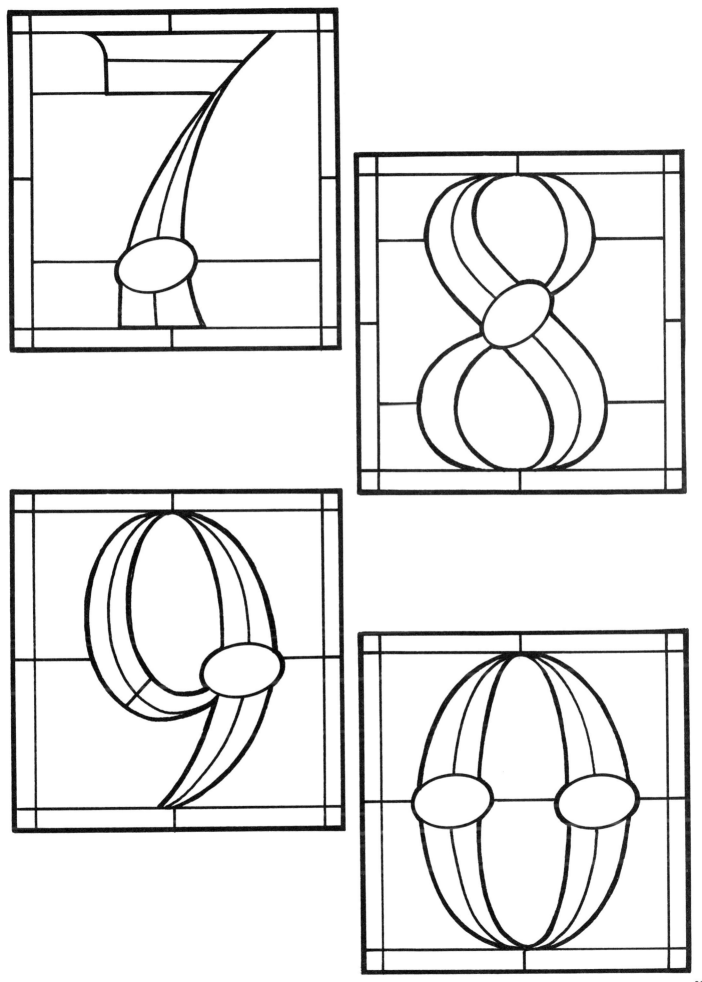

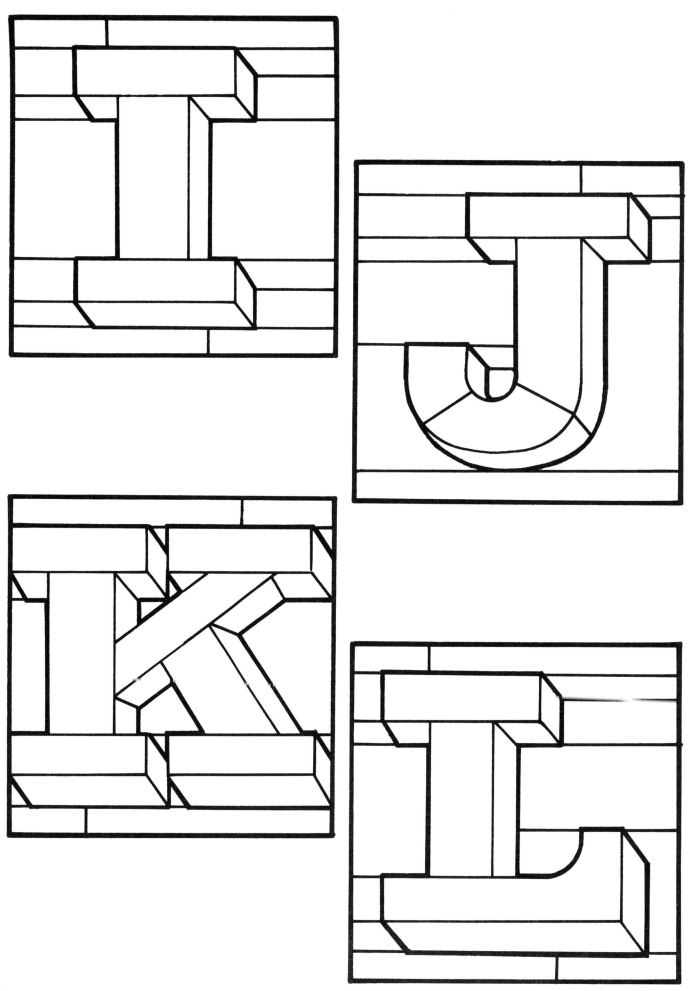

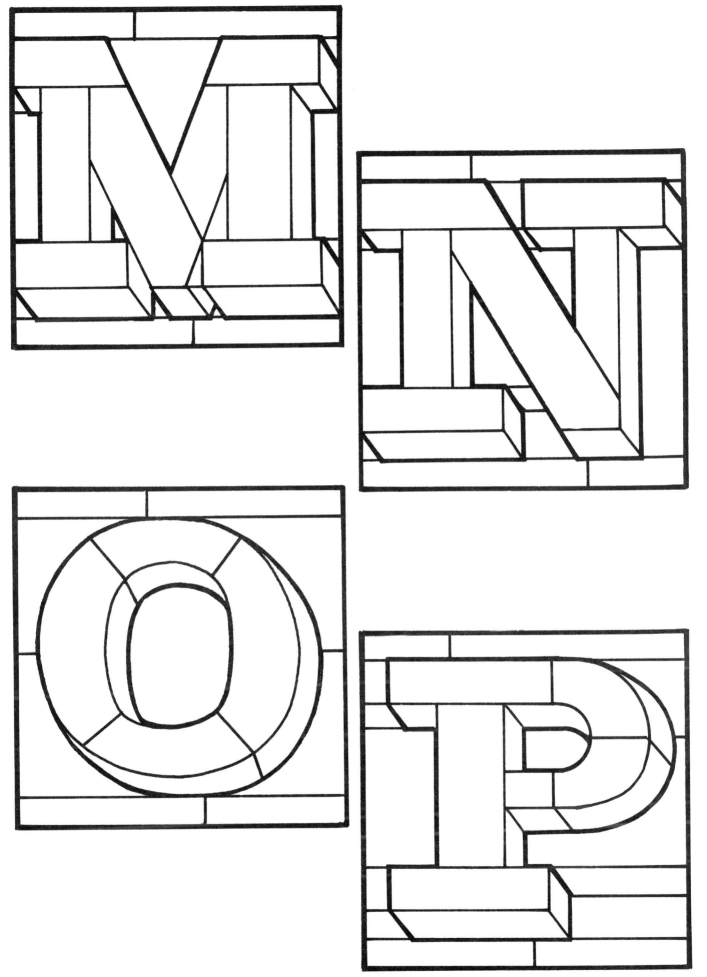

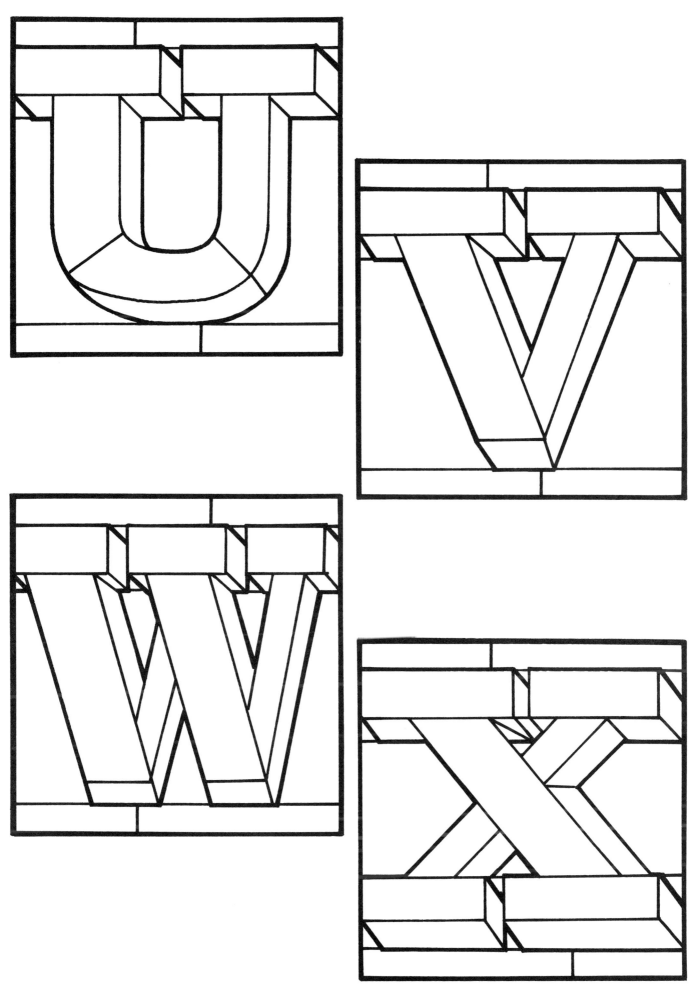

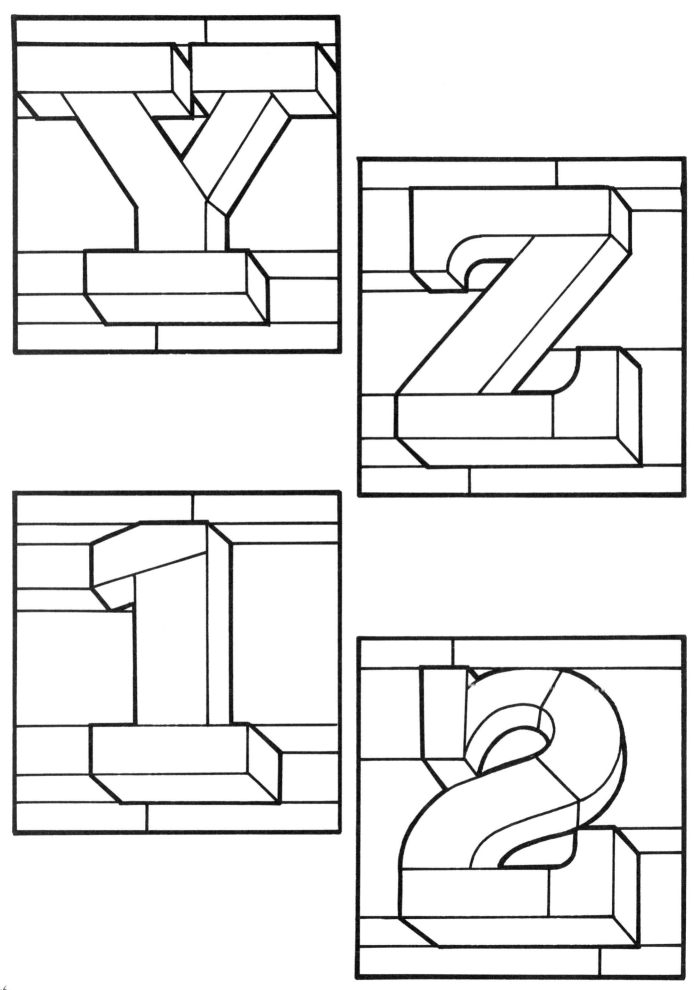

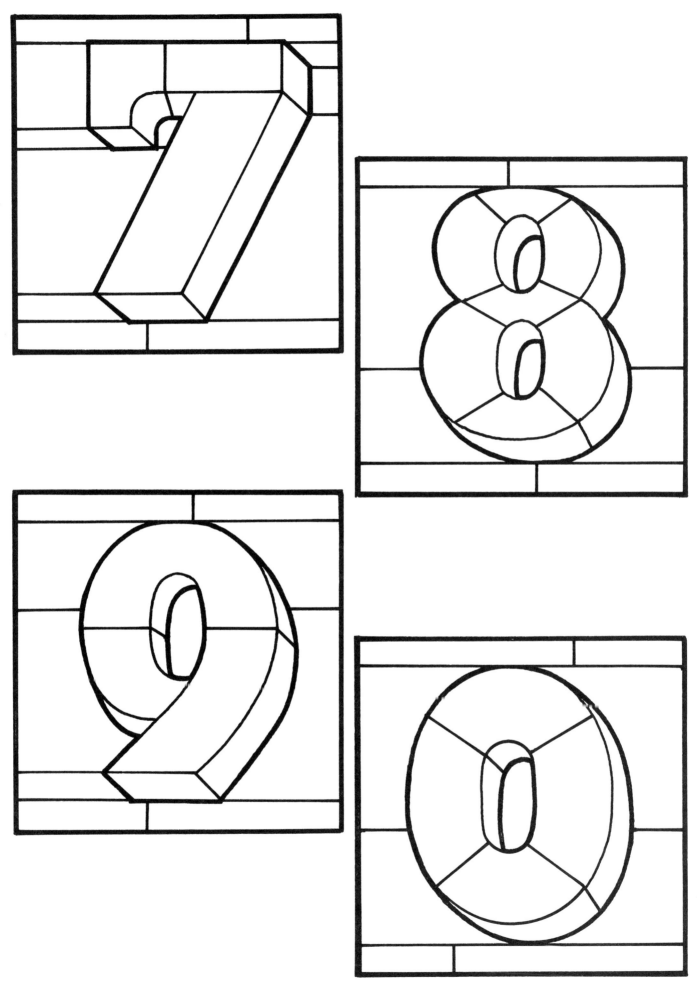

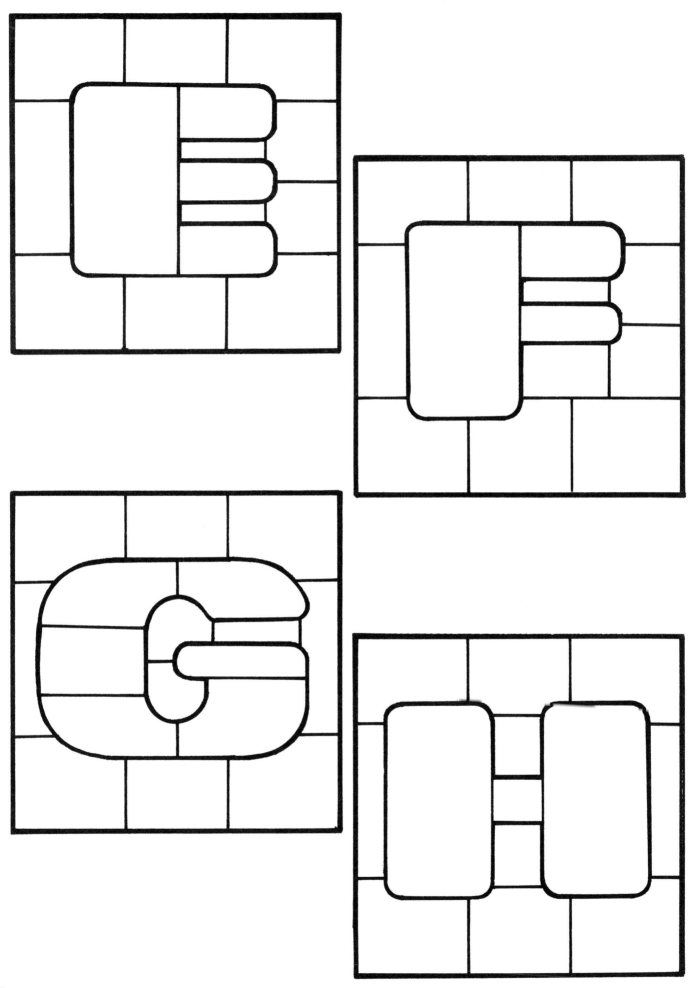

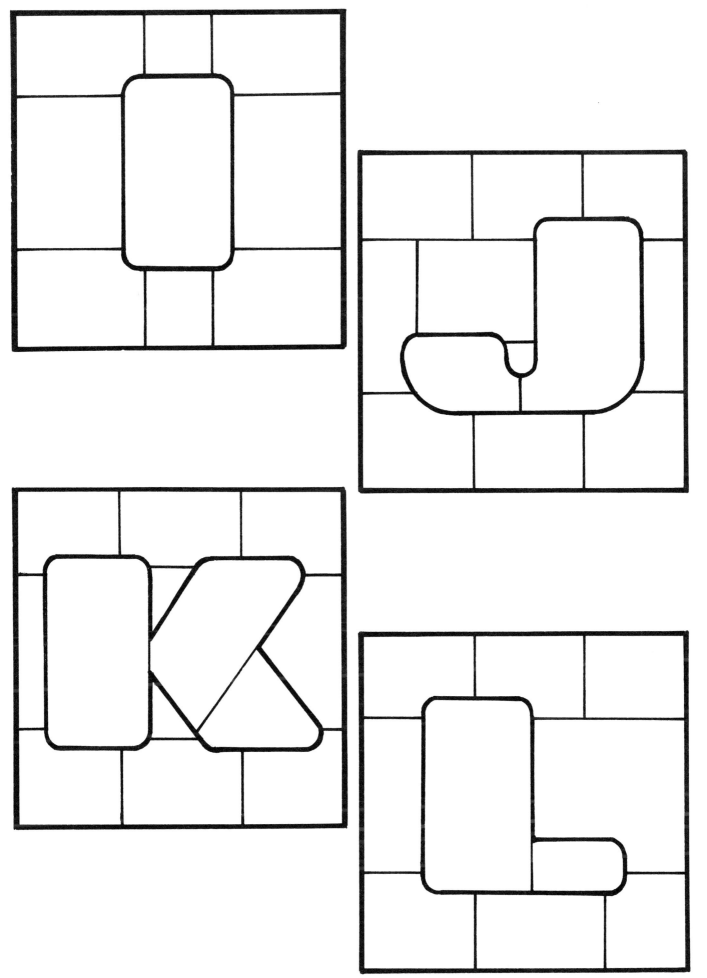

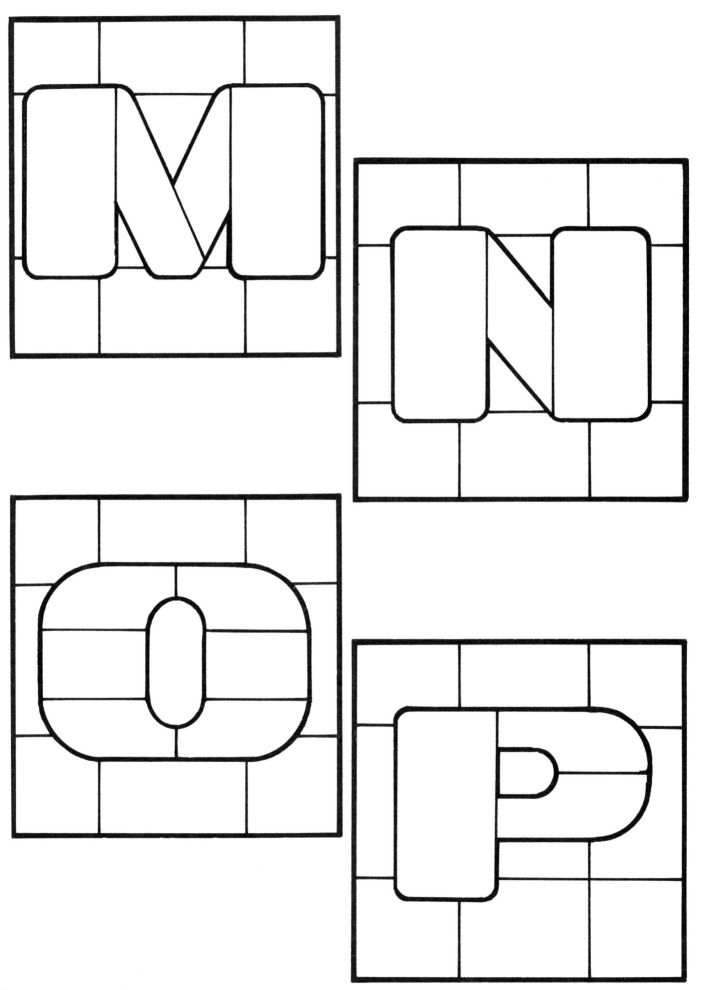

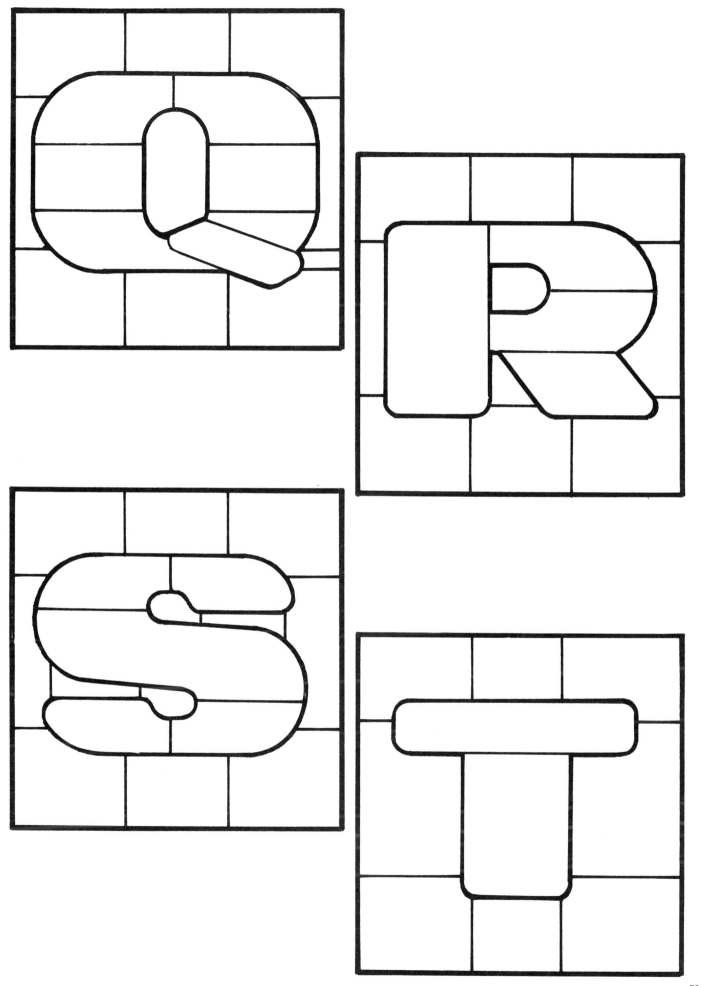

53

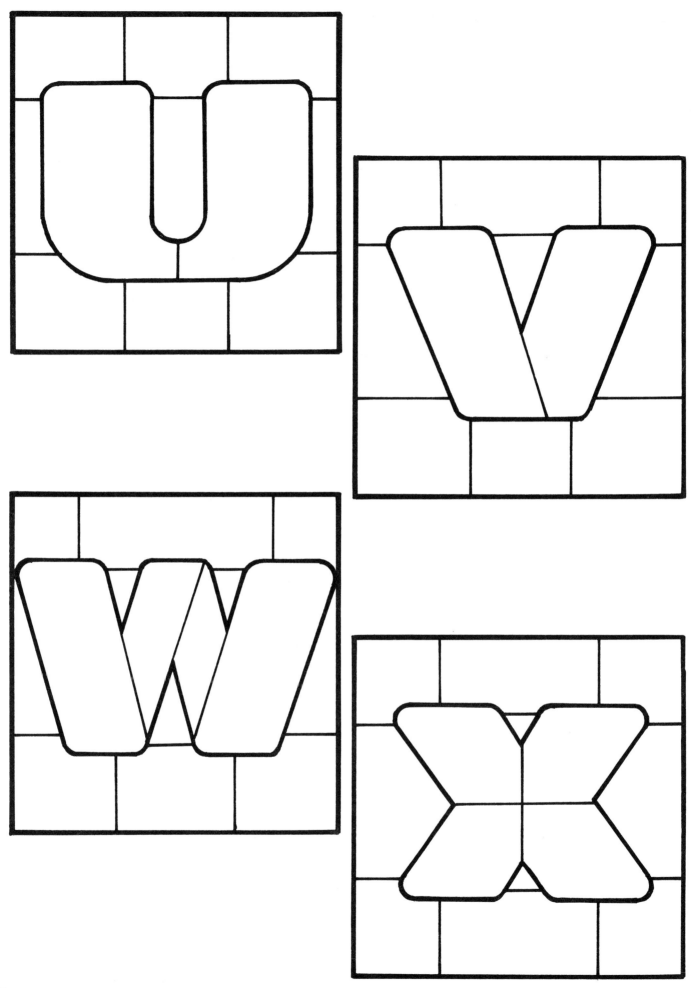

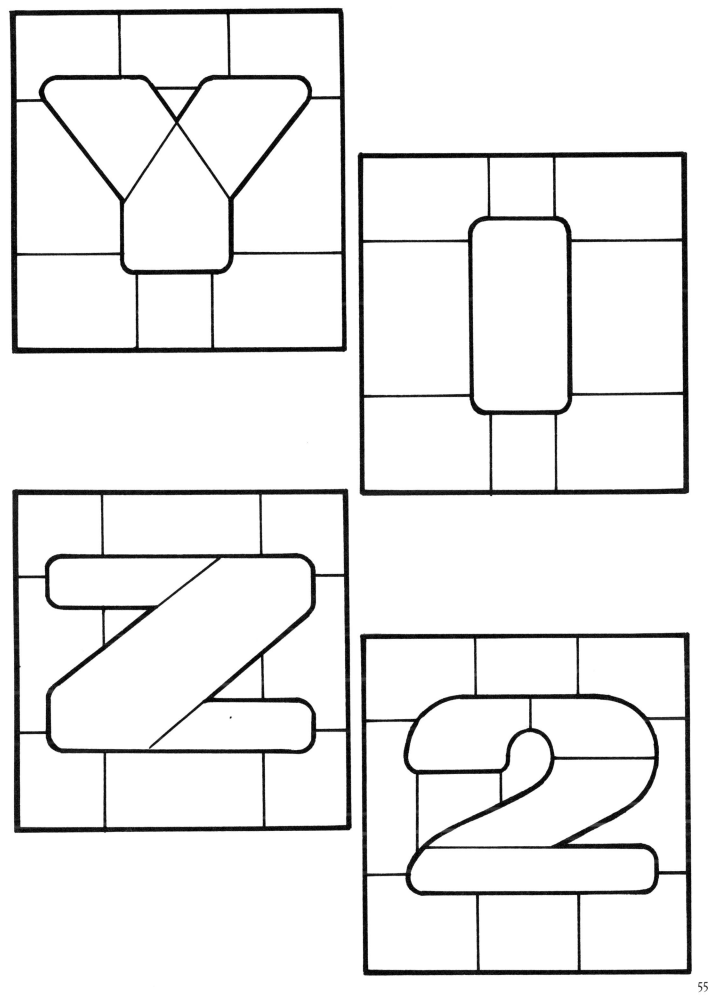

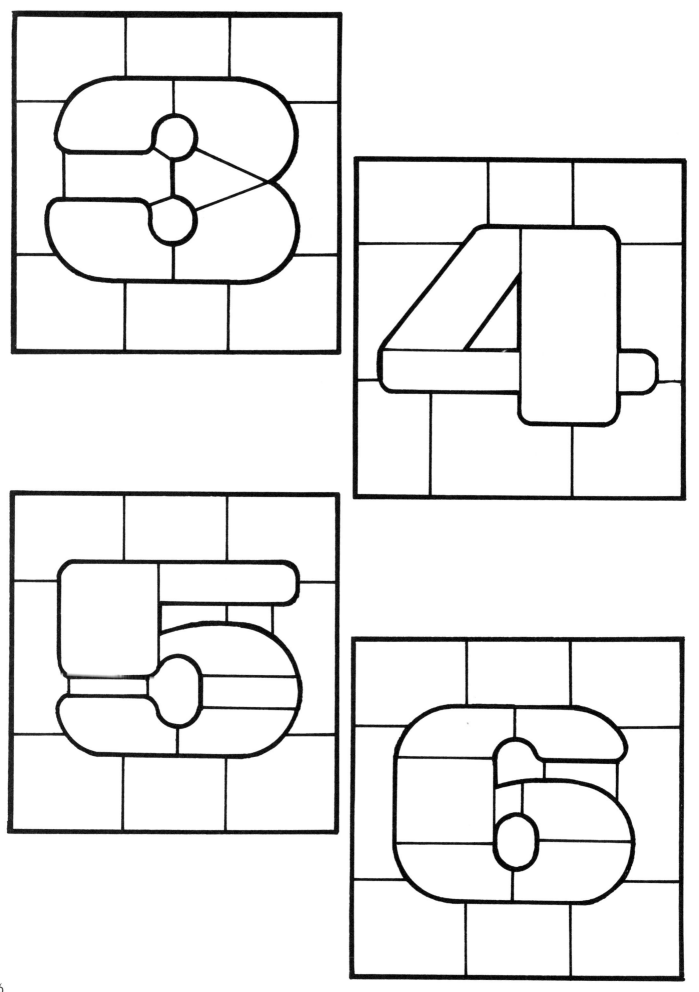

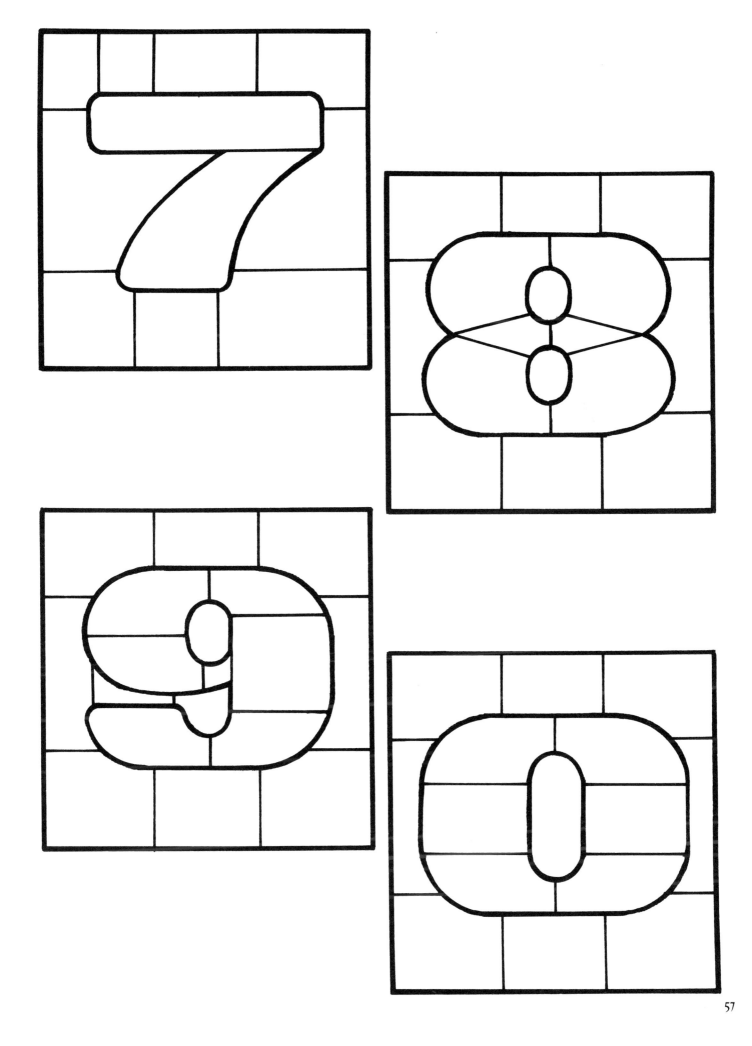

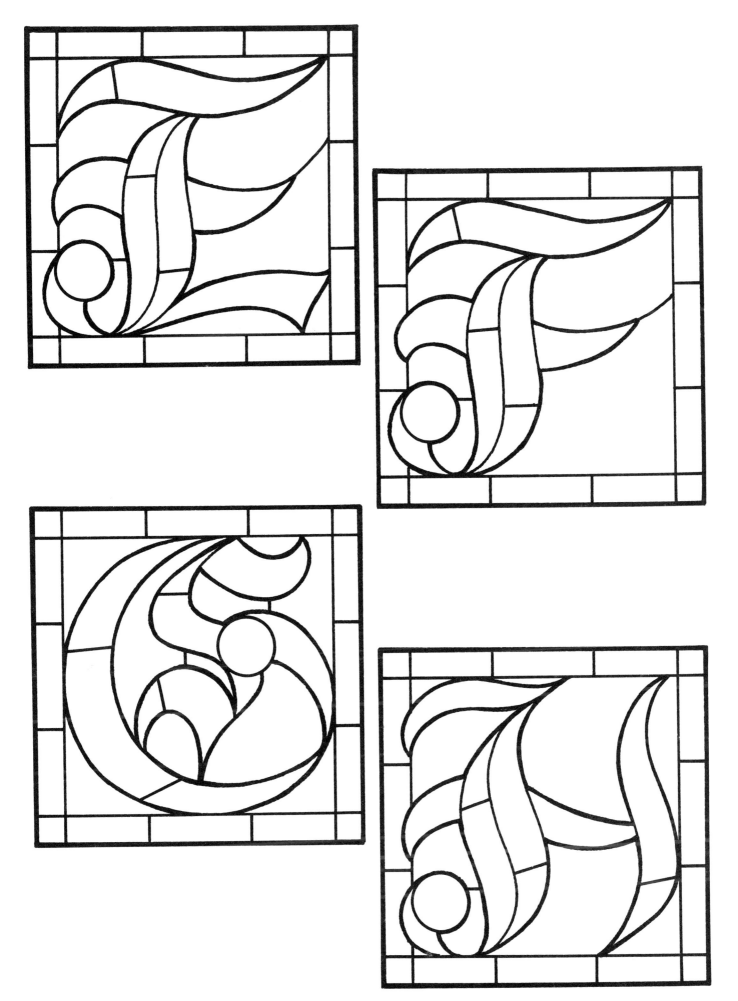